SECOND EDITION

Storybook 5

The Umbrella Book

by Sue Dickson

Illustrations by Norma Portadino, Jean Hamilton, Chip Neville and Kerstin Upmeyer

Printed in the United States of America

Modern Curriculum Press, an imprint of Pearson Learning
299 Jefferson Road, P.O. Box 480, Parsippany, NJ 07054
1-800-321-3106 / www.pearsonlearning.com

ISBN: 1-56704-515-4 (Volume 5)

G H I J K L M N—CJK—05 04 03 02 01

Raceway Step 14

ŭ

Vocabulary of 42 Words

sun
rub
mud
dull
bun
fuss
bug
nut
tub
Gus
umbrella

fun
dug
cut
must
puff
duck
cup
dump
tug
cups
dust
us
jump

hut
stuck
gum
fuzz
drum
snug
bus
up
truck
hum
mug
but

run

bud

gulp

rug

buzz

pup

Words with letters that steal another letter's sound are

RULE BREAKERS

..REVIEW VOCABULARY

tap
on
will
to
cut
have
hen
drip
left
puff
a
sip
duck

help
has
bun
pig
hop
dump
his
past
Tom
yell
pal
wet
pot

milk
tug
hot
up
was
top
bed
Tim
but
him
tan
of
hit

ă....ĕ....ĭ....ŏ....and....ŭ

Mom	as	gulp
mud	step	dog
Dad	fun	tub
the	Sam	pet
ran	jump	fuzz
dug	Max	said
Pep	us	snug
cup	give	rob
is	less	bug
ten	fuss	fed
hum	log	nut
not	did	stop
	umbrella	in

Gus

Gus is a bug.
Gus and his mom and
his dad have a hut.
It is a nut.

Gus will run to it.
Gus will puff a bit.

Gus has a big bun.

Gus has ham
on his bun.

Gus has milk.
His mom said not to gulp.
Gus will not gulp his milk.

Gus has a truck.

Gus has fun.

Gus has a drum.

Gus has jazz.

Mom said,
"It is not dull in the hut."

Gus has fun in the mud.
Gus dug and dug.

Gus dug six cups of mud.

Gus has a pal.
His pal is Max.
Gus and Max have fun
in a cup.

Gus and Max can
hum and hum.

Gus and Max can swim
in a mug.
Max can jump up and in.

Gus has an umbrella.

Will Gus get wet ?

Yes. Gus will get wet !

Gus has fun up in a bud

Gus has fun in gum,

but Gus can get stuck!

Gus must tug!

Gus must yell to get help.

Gus has fun in the sun.

If it gets hot,
Gus can get wet.

Gus will swim.

Gus and Max have
fun on a duck.

The duck will dump Gus,
and Gus will swim.

Tom has a pup.

Gus and Max hid in the fuzz of the pup.

Tom must run fast
to the bus.

Tom's pup can not run fast.

Gus said, "It is fast to us!"

Dad has a tub.

Dad will fill the tub.

Dad has cut a step in it.

Gus can get up on it.

Rub-a-dub-dub !

Dad rubs a bug in a tub.

Mom has a rug.

Fuss, fuss, fuss !

Mom will not have
dust on the rug.

Gus has a bed.

The rug is his bed.

Mom will hug a bug
in a rug.

Gus must get to bed.
Gus will get his duck.

Gus is in bed.

His duck is in bed.

Gus is snug in the fuzz
of his rug.

Gus is not sad.

Gus is glad !

The End